Great Grammar Mini-Books

by Maria Fleming

The Best Vacation Ever

A story by _Theresa Ward_
(NOUN/PERSON)

1

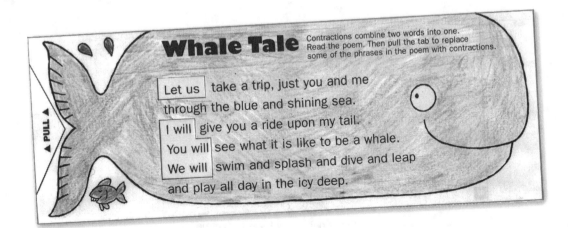

Whale Tale Contractions combine two words into one. Read the poem. Then pull the tab to replace some of the phrases in the poem with contractions.

▲ PULL ▲

Let us take a trip, just you and me
through the blue and shining sea.
I will give you a ride upon my tail.
You will see what it is like to be a whale.
We will swim and splash and dive and leap
and play all day in the icy deep.

SCHOLASTIC
PROFESSIONAL BOOKS

New York ✳ Toronto ✳ London ✳ Auckland ✳ Sydney ✳ Mexico City ✳ New Delhi ✳ Hong Kong

Teachers may photocopy the reproducible pages in this book for classroom use. No other
part of this publication may be reproduced in whole or in part, or stored in a retrieval
system, or transmitted in any form or by any means, electronic, mechanical, photocopy,
recording, or otherwise, without written permission of the publisher. For information
regarding permission, write to Scholastic Inc., 555 Broadway, New York, NY 10012.

Edited by Karen Kellaher

Cover design by Pamela Simmons

Cover photography by Donnelly Marks

Interior design by Ellen Matlach Hassell for Boultinghouse & Boultinghouse, Inc.

Cover and interior illustrations by Ellen Joy Sasaki

ISBN 0-590-18741-4

Copyright © 1999 by Maria Fleming

All rights reserved

Contents

Introduction

If a chorus of groans greets you in the classroom when you announce a lesson on grammar, then this book is for you. It's a collection of reproducible patterns for interactive mini-books designed to make grammar fun. Each book is in a special format that offers an exciting interactive component: flaps to lift, tabs to pull, wheels to turn, and more.

The first group of mini-books focuses on parts of speech, using a variety of stories and formats. For example, nouns come in handy for naming the people, places, and things that are part of a class trip; action verbs take a starring role in a mini-book "movie"; prepositions keep students hot on the trail of a lost cat in a mini-mystery. The second group of mini-books highlights grammar usage and skill development: A bevy of barnyard animals walks students through the rules for forming plurals in a lift-the-flap songbook; a turn-the-wheel riddle book allows students to practice punctuation; a visit to a pet shop turns into a lesson on how to form possessives. And that's just to mention a few!

All of the mini-books are easy to assemble. Each reproducible pattern comes with step-by-step directions for how to make the book. Teaching tips accompany each template and suggest ways to incorporate the mini-books into your grammar lessons, whether you are introducing a part of speech, reviewing a rule for usage, or reinforcing a skill.

The books offer a lively alternative—or supplement—to grammar worksheets. The interactive components of the mini-books will keep young grammarians on their toes as they hunt for certain parts of speech or search out errors in punctuation and capitalization. Best of all, the books show students grammar in action: telling a story, composing a lyric, forming a riddle, creating a poem. As a result, grammar is transformed from a dull set of rules to an exciting tool for communication. Students will come to appreciate the drama of a verb, the action-altering power of an adverb, and the decorative ability of a well-placed adjective.

We hope that these mini-books will add some zip to your grammar lessons, for you and your students. Maybe they'll even turn those groans into giggles!

Making the Mini-Books: Some General Tips

The directions for making the mini-books are not complicated; however, some are a bit more involved than others. We suggest that you assemble each book yourself before trying it as a class project. You can then walk students through the process, step-by-step, providing assistance as needed and a finished product to model.

Proper photocopying of the pattern pages is perhaps the most crucial element in constructing the books. Be sure that the alignment of a page on the copier glass is correct before you make multiple copies. It is easy to cut off part of the pattern or make a crooked copy, which may lead to imperfections in the finished book. An automatic feed slot on a copier produces the most reliable results.

Each set of directions begins with a heading marked "Preparation." You'll want to pay close attention to the photocopying instructions under this heading. Some pattern pages call for a double-sided photocopy, while others require only a single-sided copy. For best results, remove each mini-book pattern page at the perforations before copying. A photocopier with a double-sided photocopying function works best for the double-sided pages. If you are using a copier that can copy only a single side of a page at a time, be careful not to invert the pattern on the opposite side of a page as you duplicate it.

Diagrams are provided to assist you and your class in making proper cuts and folds. When beginning a mini-book project with your class, you may want to have extra copies of the pattern pages on hand in case students make mistakes in assembling the books. A little practice and patience will ensure successful results.

Nouns Take a Trip

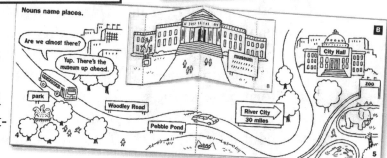

Preparation

Students will need a photocopy of pattern page 10 that includes panel B and the three pop-up strips. They will also need a double-sided photocopy of pattern pages 11 and 12 that includes panels A and C. Additional materials required are scissors, tape, glue, and crayons or markers for coloring the book.

Teaching Tips

Introduce the book to students by leading a discussion about a recent class trip (or about a trip the class will take or would like to take). Invite students to answer the following questions:

♦ Who went on the trip?

♦ Where did you go?

♦ What did you see?

As students provide answers, write the nouns they mention in three columns on the chalkboard under the headings "People," "Places," and "Things." Explain that the words in all three columns are naming words called nouns.

You might also point out that some nouns are proper (specific people, places, or things such as Mrs. Smith, United States, or Webster's Dictionary) that begin with capital letters. Other nouns are common (general people, places, or things, such as neighbor, nation, or book) that begin with lowercase letters. Although differentiating the two types of nouns is not necessary for this mini-book, students may enjoy locating examples of each noun type in the book.

To Make the Mini-Book

1. Cut along the solid lines of both pattern pages to separate panels A, B, and C and pop-up strips A, B, and C.

2. Each pop-up strip has three vertical dashed lines. Fold in along the two dashed lines at each end of the strips to create tabs. Then fold in the opposite direction along the middle dashed line, creating a mini-mountain shape with each pop-up strip.

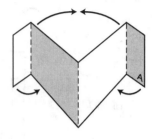

3. Take panel A and pop-up strip A (children). Tape the two end tabs of pop-up strip A onto the two boxes marked "tape tab here" on panel A.

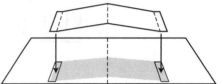

4. Repeat step 3 with pop-up strip B (museum) and panel B. Then repeat with pop-up strip C (skeletons) and panel C.

5. Fold each panel in half along the dashed vertical line. Crease well on both edges of the folded panels to flatten the pop-up strips inside.

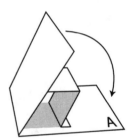

6. Stack the panels on top of one another so that the pages of the book are in order.

7. Flip the top panel (A) so that the blank side is faceup. Run a bead of glue just inside the folded edge. Flip the next panel (B) and align it neatly on top of panel A, pressing along the glue to set. Repeat with the remaining panel.

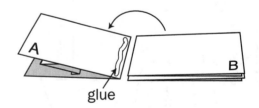

glue

9. There will be blank pages in the book. Use small dabs of glue to seal the blank pages together. First glue together the blank pages between pages 3 and 4. Then glue together the blank pages between pages 5 and 6.

Nouns name places.

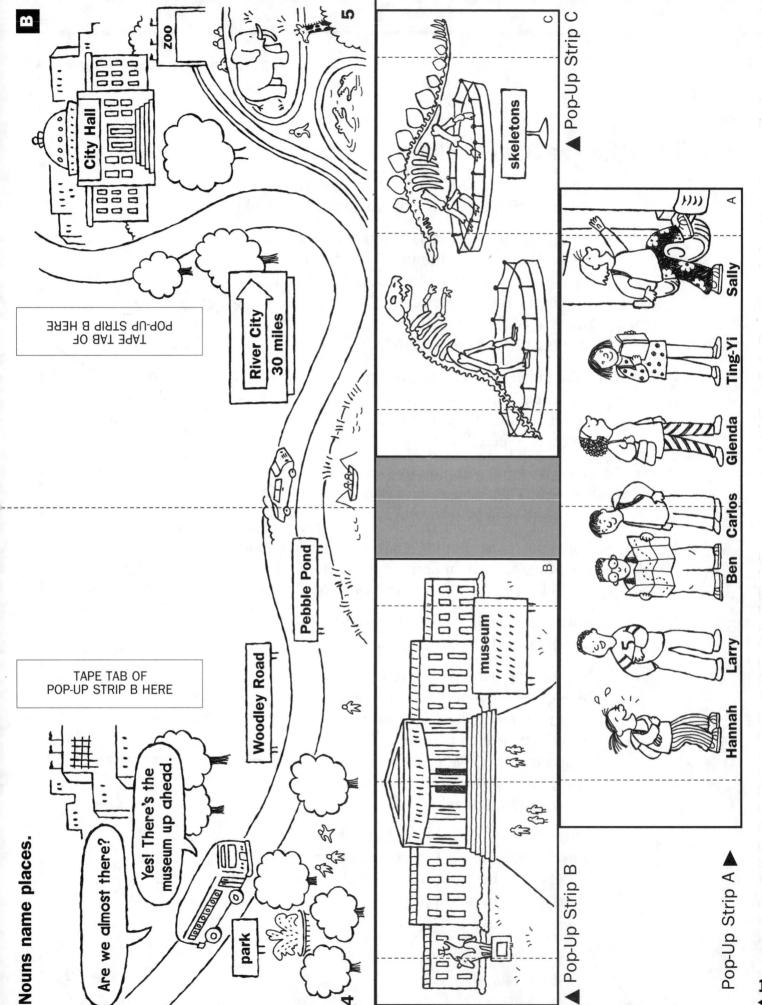

B

City Hall

ZOO

5

TAPE TAB OF
POP-UP STRIP B HERE

River City
30 miles

Woodley Road

Pebble Pond

TAPE TAB OF
POP-UP STRIP B HERE

Are we almost there?

Yes! There's the museum up ahead.

park

4

▲ Pop-Up Strip C

C

skeletons

B

museum

▲ Pop-Up Strip B

A

Hannah   Larry   Ben   Carlos   Glenda   Ting-Yi   Sally

Pop-Up Strip A ▶

1

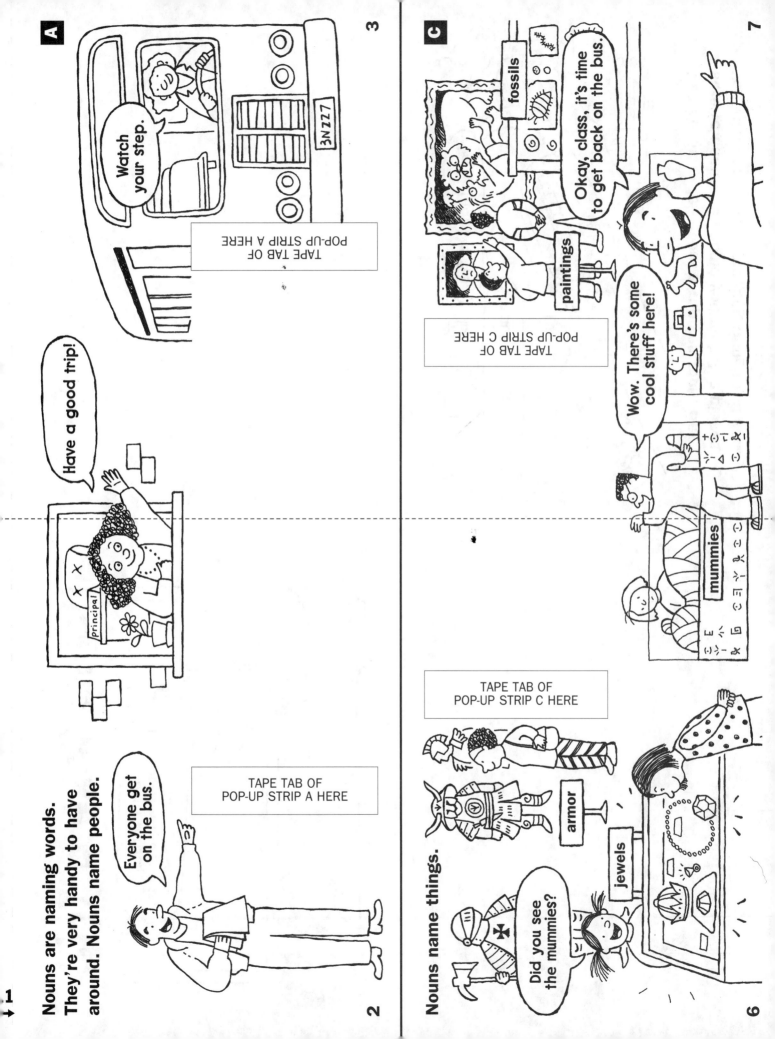

Use nouns to tell about a trip you took. Be sure to name the people you met, the places you went, and the interesting things you saw.

Wow! That was fun.

When can we go back?

Great Grammar Mini-Books Scholastic Professional Books

Nouns Take a Trip

Don't forget. Tomorrow is our class trip to the museum!

Superdog to the Rescue!

Preparation

Provide each student with a copy of the patterns on page 15. Students will also need scissors, tape, glue, oak tag, and crayons or markers for coloring the book.

Teaching Tips

Explain to students that many verbs are action words. After students finish making their books and viewing the action-adventure "movie," ask them to replay it beginning with the first screen. How many verbs can they find?

When students are through with the mini-movie and verb search, have them make their own verb-packed films. Students should cut the paper strip along one of the taped edges. They can then pull the strip out, flip it over, and use the reverse side to write and illustrate their own action adventure movie. Challenge students to use as many action verbs as they can in their movies.

Be sure to point out to students that not all verbs are action words; provide examples of verbs that express a condition or state of being (for example: *is, will, am*) to help students distinguish among the different types of verbs.

To Make the Mini-Book

1. Cut out panels A and B along the solid lines.

2. Tape the end of panel A to the beginning of panel B to create one long strip. The first box on the strip should be the movie title, *Superdog to the Rescue.* The last box should say, "The End."

3. Cut out the movie theater along the outer solid lines. Paste the movie theater onto a piece of oak tag cut to size.

4. Carefully cut along the inner solid lines (students may need adult assistance to make these interior cuts). You should have a cutaway box (the "movie screen") and two slits running alongside it.

5. Thread the long strip through the slits. Begin by placing the strip on the desk so that the pictures and text are right-side-up. Push the right edge of the strip through the front of the slit on the left side of the cutaway box. Pull the strip behind the cutaway box so that the pictures and text are visible through it. Then push the strip through the back of the slit on the right side of the cut-away box. Pull it through a few inches.

6. Align the free ends of the strip and tape them together to create one continuous loop.

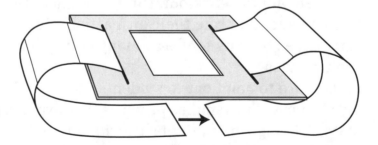

7. Pull the strip to the left until the movie title is visible through the cutaway screen.

8. To view the movie, continue pulling the strip to the left, box by box.

Superdog to the Rescue!

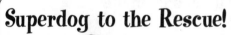

An Action-Adventure Movie Starring SUPERDOG, a Helpless Kitten, and Lots of Verbs

Superdog heard an urgent call for help.

Superdog climbed the tree.

A

She swung onto the ledge.

She grabbed the kitten.

Superdog jumped to safety.

THE END

Adjectives Are Awesome

Preparation

Provide each student with a double-sided copy of "Adjectives Are Awesome" (pages 17 and 18). Students will also need scissors, pencils, and crayons or markers for coloring the book.

Teaching Tips

Explain to students that adjectives are words that describe nouns. To point out how adjectives dress up nouns, invite students to draw pictures of the following:

♦ a sneaker

♦ a high-topped, purple, polka-dotted, rainbow-laced sneaker

Ask: *Which was easier to imagine? Which picture has more detail?* Students can further explore adjectives' descriptive powers by assembling and reading the mini-book. When they've read the mini-book, encourage students to come up with additional "plain noun" sentences. They can then ask partners to dress up the sentences with adjectives.

To Make the Mini-Book

1. Place the page on the desk so that side B faces up.

2. Fold the edges of the pages in along the vertical dashed lines. Crease well.

3. Cut along each solid line.

4. Open the flaps to reveal a new sentence after reading each sentence on the front of the book.

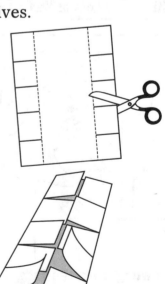

Are Awesome

plain old nouns
them up.
to see how
add details
sentence
to life.

saw a house.

did a trick.

found a frog.

up this sentence
fabulous adjectives.
under the flaps.

bought a hat.

Adjectives

Adjectives take
and dress
Open the flaps
adjectives can
that make a
come

The boy

The dog

The girl

Now you try. Dress
with some
Write your sentence

The woman

Great Grammar Mini-Books Scholastic Professional Books

Hooray for wonderful adjectives!

The **terrified** boy saw a **haunted** house.

The **huge**, **shaggy** dog did an **amazing** trick.

Hi, I'm Fred the Frog. I can grant you three wishes.

The **surprised** girl found a **magic** frog.

The _____ woman bought a _____ hat.

Draw a picture to go with your new sentence.

An Adverb Works Hard

Preparation

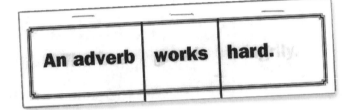

Make photocopies of pages 21 and 22 for each student. The copies should be two separate sheets rather than one double-sided page. Students will also need scissors and staplers.

Teaching Tips

After helping students assemble the books, ask them to flip through the pages. Ask them if they can identify the parts of speech in each sentence. All of the sentences have the same simple construction (noun-verb-adverb). If students are being introduced to adverbs for the first time, tell them that the third word in each sentence is called an adverb. Explain that adverbs describe verbs the way adjectives describe nouns; adverbs tell us *how* something is done. Ask students what they notice about most of the adverbs in the book. Then mention that their common ending, the letters *ly*, is often (but not always!) a sign that the word is an adverb.

Have students flip through the pages of the book with the sentences uncut. Then ask them to cut along the dashed line on each page separating the verb and adverb. Have them flip through the pages randomly this time, mixing and matching adverbs with subject/predicate phrases. Encourage students to focus on how the introduction of a new adverb changes the way each action is performed. Now have students cut along the dashed line on each page separating the noun and verb, and flip through the pages randomly again, mixing up the nouns, verbs, and adverbs and forming silly sentences. Have students make lists of sentences that make sense and sentences that are nonsensical.

After students experiment with the mini-book, point out that adverbs can also tell when, where, or to what degree. Mention also that adverbs can modify adjectives and other adverbs, in addition to verbs. For example, in the sentence "the Great Lakes are very beautiful," the word *very* is an adverb modifying the adjective *beautiful*.

To Make the Mini-Book

1. Cut apart the panels along the solid lines on each page.

2. Place the panels in a neat stack. The panel that reads "An adverb works hard" should be on top of the stack. The order of the rest of the panels does not matter.

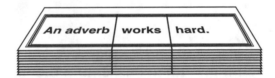

3. Staple along the top edge of the stack of panels to create a booklet.

4. Cut along the solid lines on each panel to separate the sentences into noun, verb, and adverb segments. Be careful not to cut all the way to the stapled edge, or the pages will come apart.

5. Flip the noun, verb, and adverb segments to create silly sentences.

| An adverb | works | hard. |

| The bear | growls | hungrily. |

| The moon | shines | brightly. |

| The man | sings | sweetly. |

| The tree | grows | slowly. |

21

The fish	swims	gracefully.
The kite	dances	wildly.
The pig	squeals	joyfully.
The boy	smiles	shyly.
The flower	blooms	beautifully.

Great Grammar Mini-Books Scholastic Professional Books

Where Is Foofy?

Preparation

Provide each student with a double-sided photocopy of reproducibles A and B (pages 25–26) and a double-sided photocopy of reproducibles C and D (pages 27–28). Students will also need scissors and crayons or markers for coloring the book.

Teaching Tips

Help students identify prepositions in a piece of classroom reading. Tell them that prepositions are small words that have big jobs; they often tell the reader where something is. Write some "locating" prepositions on the chalkboard, such as *in, out, over, through, with,* and so on. Encourage students to use the words to help identify objects around the room, for example, *The crayons are on the floor. The clock is over the door.*

To Make the Mini-Book

1. Take page A. Cut along all the solid lines.

2. Turn the page over so that the side B is faceup. Fold the page in half along the horizontal dashed line, bringing the top of the page down. Then fold it in half again along the vertical dashed line.

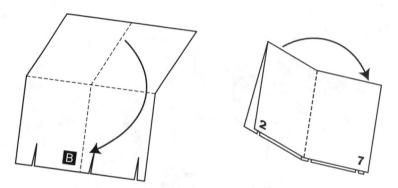

3. Repeat steps 1 and 2 with page C.

4. Take the folded section that has page C facing up and nest it inside the page A section. Double-check the mini-book page numbers to make sure they are in order.

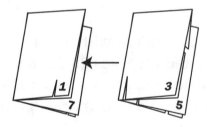

5. Staple the book along the left edge to hold the pages together.

6. As you read the story, lift the flaps to search for Foofy.

Where could Foofy be?

Where is Foofy?
Follow the prepositions
to solve this kitty caper.

Aha, there's Foofy! She's on the
table, visiting the fish. Good Foofy!

"Hey, Furball, why don't you take a long walk off a short pier?"

"Meow."

**Now read the story again.
Can you find six prepositions?
Circle them all. Lift this flap
to check your answers.**

A

Great Grammar Mini-Books Scholastic Professional Books

Where Is Foofy?

page 3: under   page 4: behind   page 5: in
page 6: up   page 8: on, off

Great Grammar Mini-Books Scholastic Professional Books

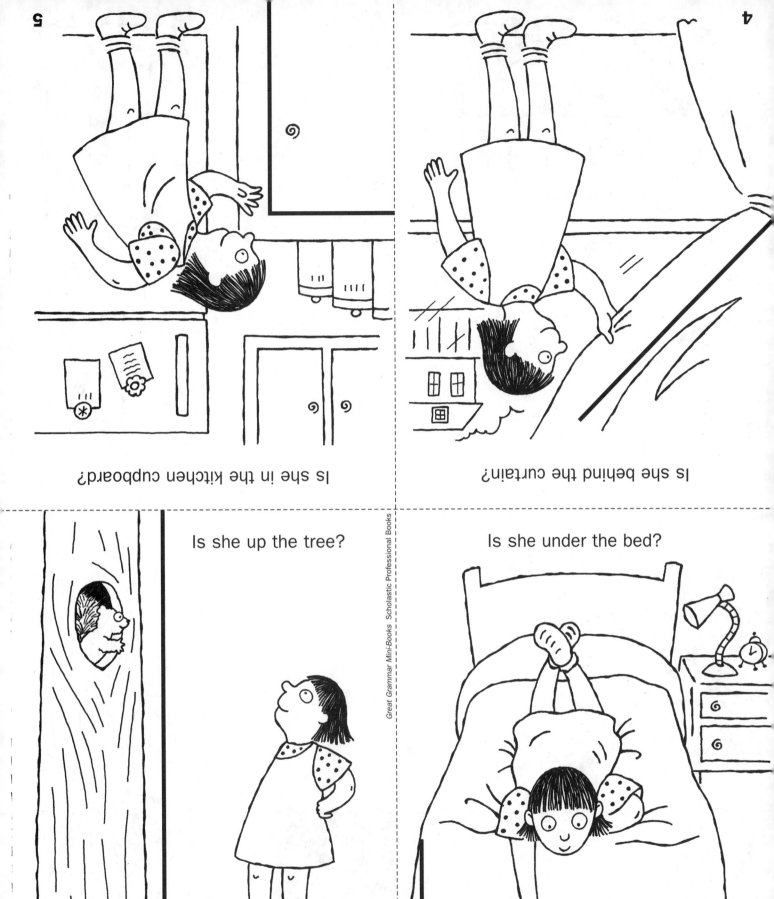

Is she behind the curtain?

Is she in the kitchen cupboard?

Is she under the bed?

Is she up the tree?

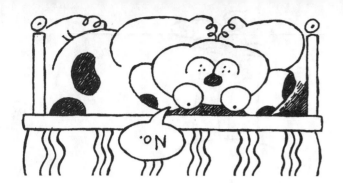

Great Grammar Mini-Books Scholastic Professional Books

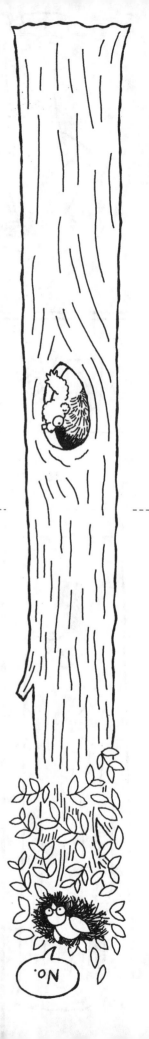

D

2

The Best Vacation Ever

Preparation

Divide students into pairs and provide each pair with a double-sided photocopy of pages 31–32. Students will also need scissors, a stapler, a pencil, and crayons or markers to complete the activity.

Teaching Tips

This wacky fill-in-the-blanks book will help you review the parts of speech with students. The mini-book includes a basic story line, but some of the words have been deleted. Students will work together to fill in the missing parts of speech to create a silly story.

After pairs of students have made the mini-books, have each student choose a role: One will be the "clue giver" and one will be the "parts of speech provider." Have the clue giver hold the book and read through it silently. The clue giver should stop periodically to ask his or her partner to provide the appropriate part of speech for each blank space in the text, then write the word on the empty line. After the clue giver has written in all of his or her partner's word selections, the two students can go back to page one and read the text aloud together. Invite students to use this mini-book as a model for creating their own fill-in-the-blanks books focusing on parts of speech.

Note: Students will need to understand the difference between past- and present-tense verbs to use this mini-book.

To Make the Mini-Book

1. Place the page on the desk so that panels A and B are faceup.

2. Cut the panels apart along the solid lines.

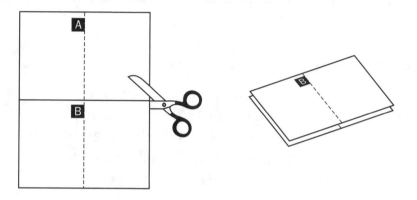

3. Put panel B on top of panel A.

4. Fold in along the dashed line. Double-check the mini-book page numbers to make sure they are in order.

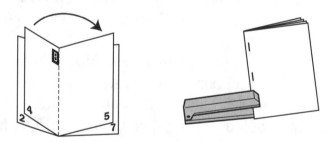

5. Staple along the left edge of the book to hold the pages together.

The Best Vacation Ever

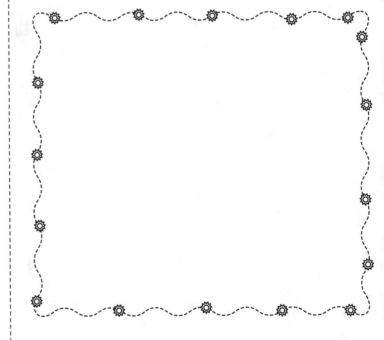

A story by _____.
(NOUN/PERSON)

1

Great Grammar Mini-Books Scholastic Professional Books

They would like to _____ in
(VERB/PRESENT TENSE)

_____, where they can
(NOUN/PLACE)

_____ under the stars and
(VERB)

roast _____ over an open fire.
(NOUN/PLURAL)

8

They packed plenty of _____
(NOUN/PLURAL)

and _____ in their suitcases
(NOUN/PLURAL)

and hopped _____ on a plane.
(ADVERB)

3

Before they went home, they went to

_____. They bought
(NOUN/PLACE)

a _____ _____ and
(ADJECTIVE)   (NOUN/THING)

a _____ _____.
(ADJECTIVE)   (NOUN/THING)

6

A

Great Grammar Mini-Books Scholastic Professional Books

Last summer, _____
(NOUN/PERSON)

and _____ went to
(NOUN/PERSON)

_____ for a vacation.
(NOUN/PLACE)

2

"These will make _____
(ADJECTIVE)

souvenirs for _____," they
(NOUN/PERSON)

said _____. On the way home,
(ADVERB)

they planned their vacation for next year.

7

B

At the _____, they met
(NOUN/PLACE)

their friends _____ and
(NOUN/PERSON)

_____.
(NOUN/PERSON)

4

The four friends had a _____
(ADJECTIVE)

time. They _____ _____
(VERB/PAST TENSE)   (ADVERB)

in the ocean and _____
(VERB/PAST TENSE)

_____ on the beach.
(ADVERB)

5

Old MacDonald's Mixed-Up Farm

Preparation

Provide each student with double-sided photocopies of pattern page A (pages 35–36) and pattern page B (pages 37–38). Students will also need staplers, pencils, and crayons or markers.

Teaching Tips

Each page of this mini-book reviews one of the rules for forming plurals and provides an example of that rule in action. After students read the book, you may want to divide them into small groups and have them generate lists of other words that follow the five rules for forming plurals that are included in the book. Compile the lists into a class master list of plurals.

The five basic rules for making plurals are:

♦ Add *s* to the end of most singular nouns.

♦ Add *es* to the end of a singular noun ending in *ch, sch, s, sh, x,* or *z.*

♦ Drop the *y* and add *ies* to a singular noun ending in a consonant followed by *y.*

♦ Memorize odd plurals, in which the word changes altogether (*man/men, foot/feet*).

♦ Remember plurals in which the word does not change at all (*sheep/sheep, deer/deer*).

How to Make the Mini-Book:

1. Begin by placing pattern page A faceup on the desk. Cut the page along the solid horizontal line to create two panels.

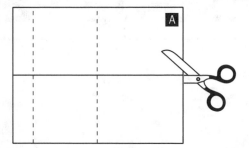

2. Fold the edge of each panel in along the dashed vertical line at its far left edge. Crease sharply to keep the folds in place.

3. Flip the panels over. Again, fold the edge of each panel in along the dashed vertical line at its far left edge. Crease sharply to keep the folds in place.

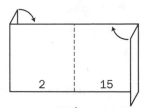

4. Now fold each panel in half along the dashed vertical lines.

5. Place pattern page B faceup on the desk. Repeat steps 1–4 with this page.

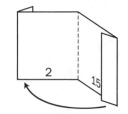

6. Now nest the folded panels inside one another so that the book pages are in numerical order. Be sure each panel's edges are creased properly so that they remain folded.

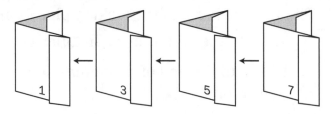

7. Staple along the left edge of the book to hold the pages in place. As you read the book, lift the folded edges of the pages to reveal the plural form of each type of animal.

Old MacDonald's Mixed-Up Farm

E-I E-I O!

1

On that farm he had some penguins.

E-I-E-I-O

3

Great Grammar Mini-Books Scholastic Professional Books

Check your answers from pages 12 and 14. Then review the plurals by filling in the blanks.

The plural of pig is PIGS, in case anyone's interested.

one gorilla   many gorillas

one platypus   many platypuses

one penguin   many _____

one ostrich   many _____

one wallaby   many _____

one mouse   many _____

one moose   many _____

16

a platypus.

Try again! Write the plural of **platypus** on the line under the flap on the next page.

14

a gorilla.

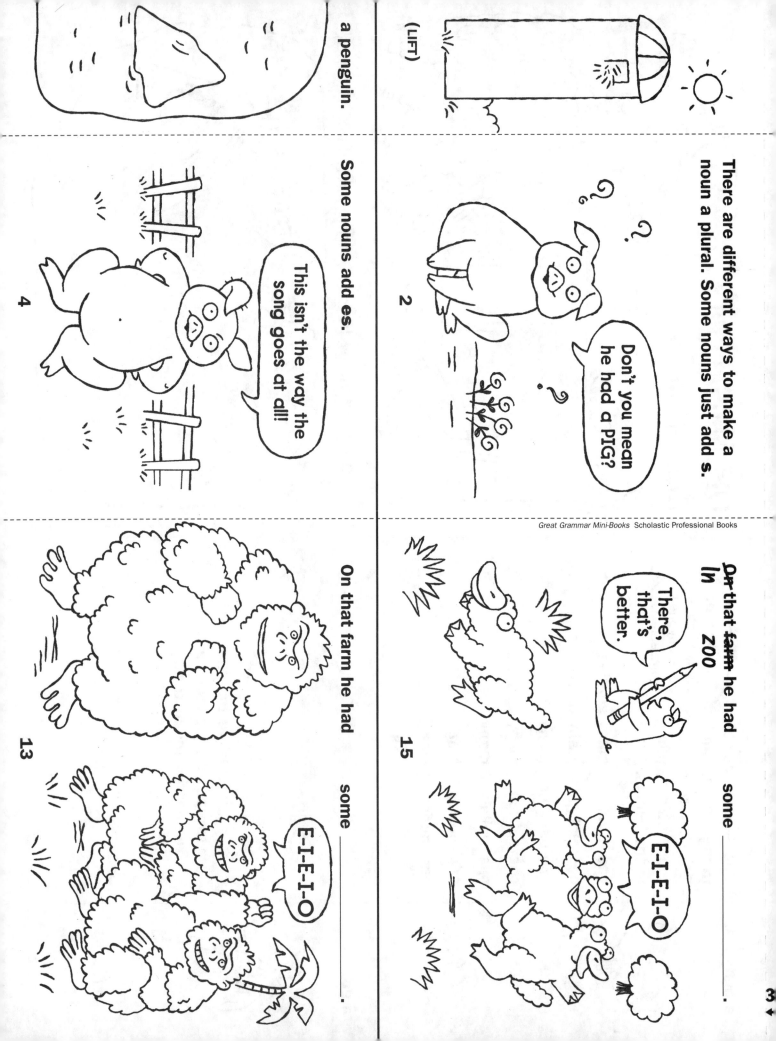

a penguin.

(LIFT)

There are different ways to make a noun a plural. Some nouns just add s.

2

Don't you mean he had a PIG?

Some nouns add es.

4

This isn't the way the song goes at all!

Great Grammar Mini-Books Scholastic Professional Books

On that farm he had In zoo

There, that's better.

some _____.

E-I-E-I-O

15

some _____.

On that farm he had

13

some _____.

E-I-E-I-O

3

B

some ostriches.

E-I-E-I-O

On that farm he had

5

some wallabies.

E-I-E-I-O

On that farm he had

7

a moose.

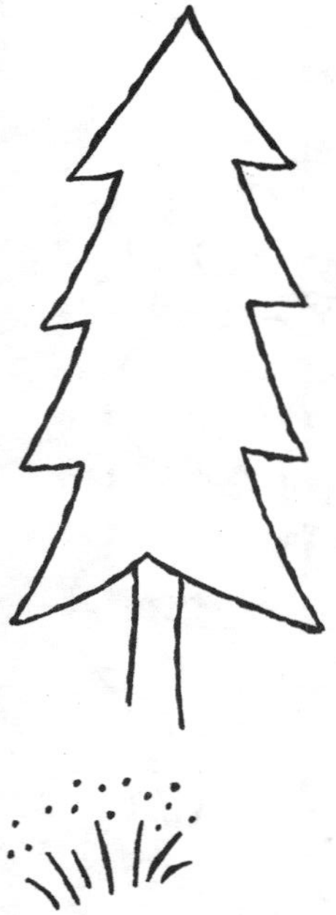

Now you try. Write the plural of **gorilla** on the line under the flap on the next page.

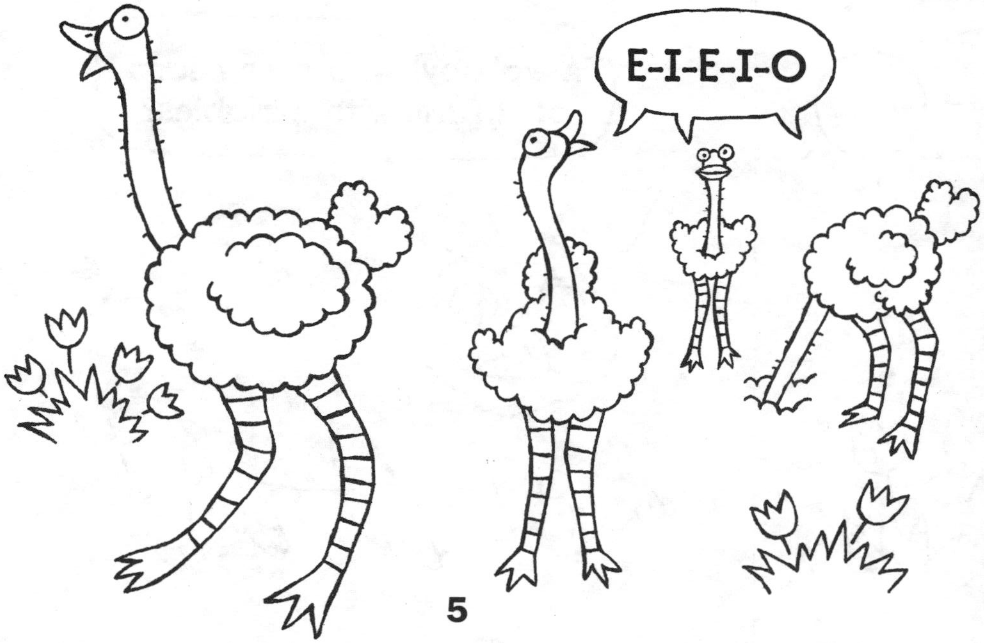

12

a mouse.

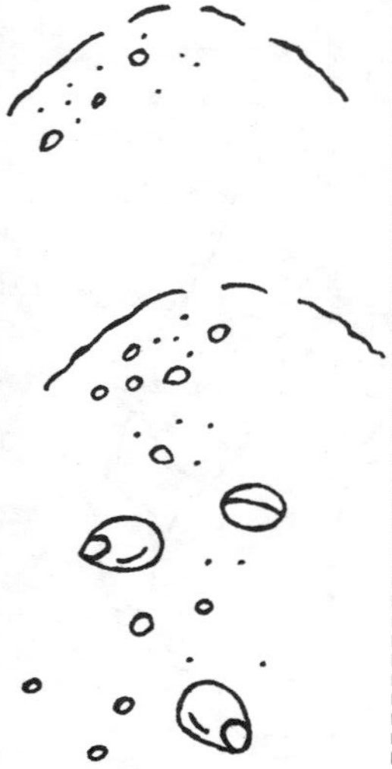

And some words don't change at all.

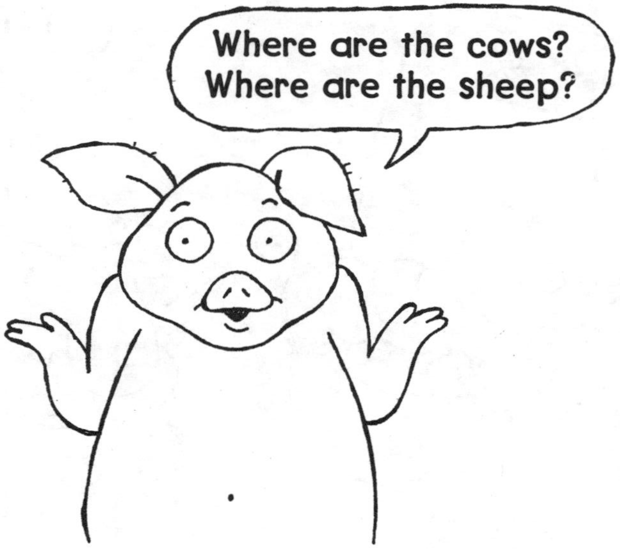

Where are the cows?
Where are the sheep?

10

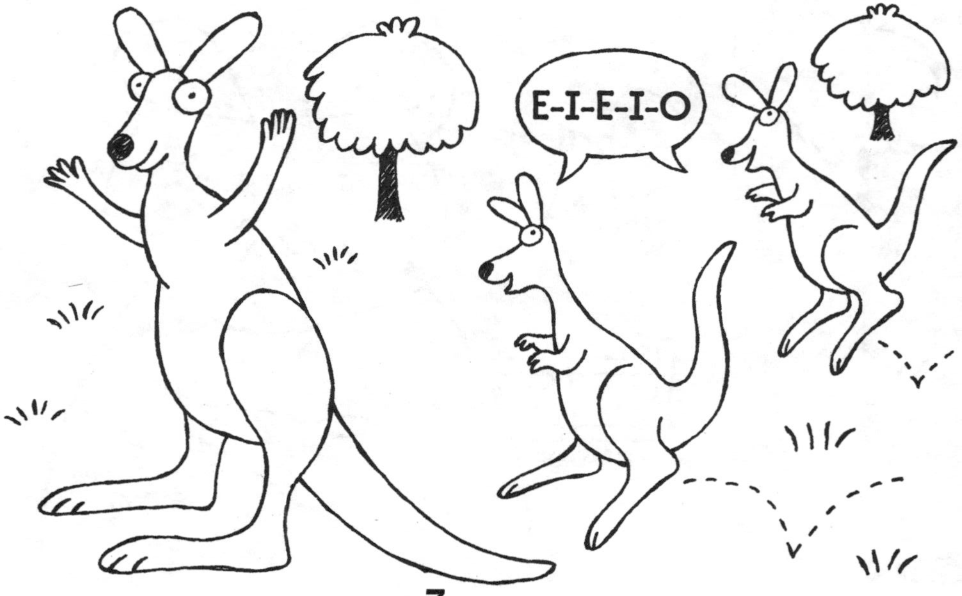

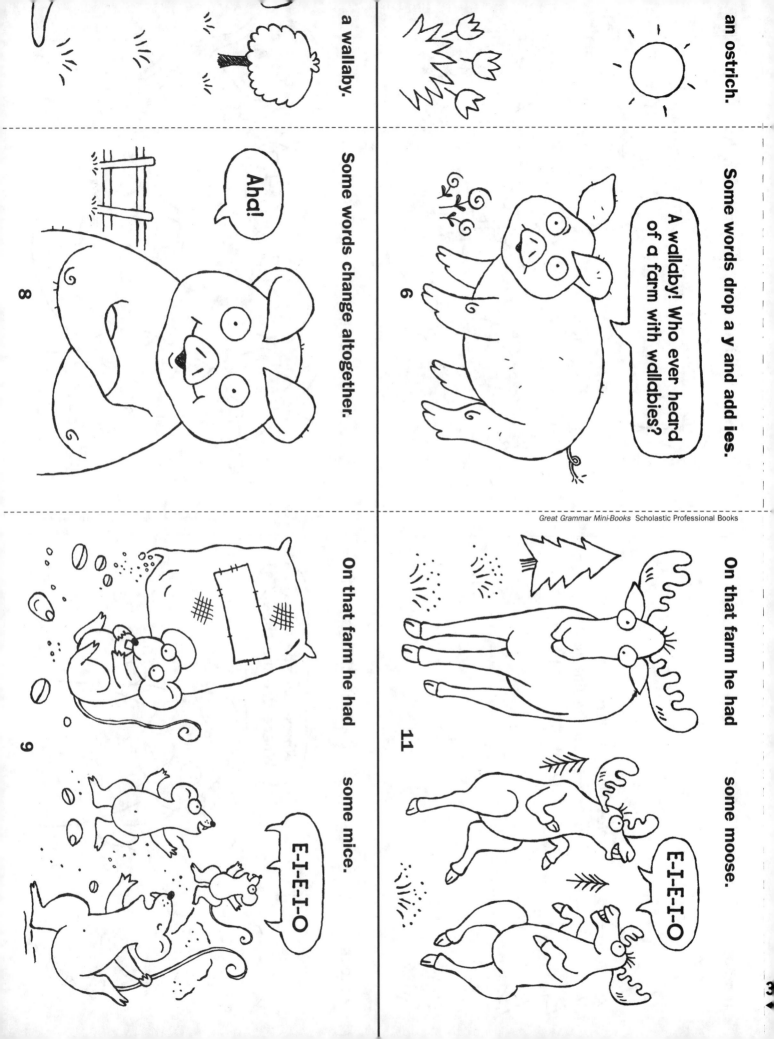

an ostrich.

a wallaby.

Some words drop a y and add ies.

A wallaby! Who ever heard of a farm with wallabies?

6

Some words change altogether.

Aha!

8

On that farm he had some moose.

E-I-E-O

11

On that farm he had some mice.

E-I-E-O

9

Preparation

Provide each student with single-sided copies of pattern pages A and B (pages 41 and 42) and pattern page C (page 43). Students will also need scissors, a stapler, three brass fasteners, and crayons or markers for coloring the book.

Teaching Tips

This mini-book concentrates on comma placement for items in a series and on end punctuation. You may want to review these punctuation rules before students read this riddle wheel book. These rules are:

♦ A comma separates items in a list of three or more items. You do not use a comma to separate two items. For example: *He bought a hat, a coat, and some new shoes.* BUT: *He bought a hat and a coat.*

♦ There are three sentence enders. A period (.) ends a declarative sentence. A question mark (?) ends an interrogative sentence. An exclamation point (!) ends an exclamatory sentence (*I won!*) or a strong imperative sentence (*Go away!*).

As a follow-up activity, create an illustrated class big book of "knock-knock" jokes to demonstrate and practice proper punctuation for quotations.

How to Make the Mini-Book:

1. Cut out circles 3, 5, and 7 on pattern page C.

2. Cut along the solid lines to remove a section of each wheel.

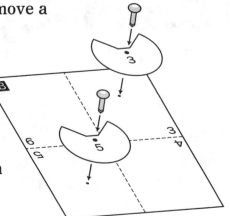

3. Place pattern page B on the desk. Align wheel 3 over dot 3 on page 3 of the mini-book. Use a brass fastener to hold the wheel in place on the page. Then attach wheel 5 to page 5 of the mini-book using a brass fastener.

4. Place pattern page A on the desk. Attach wheel 7 to page 7 of the mini-book using a brass fastener.

5. Place pattern page A on the desk so that the blank side of the page faces up. Fold the page in half, folding the top of the page down to meet the bottom. Fold the page in half again along the vertical dashed line.

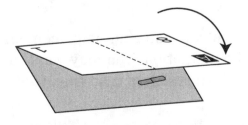 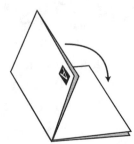

6. Repeat step 5 with pattern page B.

7. Nest folded page B inside folded page A so that the pages of the mini-book are in numerical order. Staple along the left edge of the book to hold the pages together.

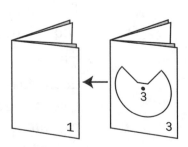

8. Turn the wheels as you read the mini-book to find the riddle that uses the correct punctuation.

A

A man on a horse holding a chicken.

The riddle with the correct punctuation is 1.

8

Animal Crack-Ups

What did the sheep say to the pig who could not keep a secret?

You're such a squealer!

Great Grammar Mini-Books Scholastic Professional Books

1

7

Which riddle has the correct punctuation?
Write the number here: _____

3.
What has 2 arms
2 wings, 2 tails 3 heads,
3 bodies and 8 legs?

2.
What has
2 arms, 2
wings, 2 tails,
3 heads,
3 bodies,
and 8 legs?

4.
What has,
2 arms, 2
wings, 2 tails.
3 heads,
3 bodies,
and 8 legs?

1.
What has 2 arms,
2 wings, 2 tails,
3 heads, 3 bodies,
and 8 legs?

2

It's been nice gnawing you.

What did the beaver say to the tree?

Each of those pages to find the riddle that uses the correct punctuation.

In this book, you will find riddles that challenge your brain and tickle your funny bone. But there's a trick. The riddles on pages 3, 5, and 7 are written four different ways. Turn the wheel on each of those pages to find the riddle that uses the correct punctuation.

B

Cockle-poodle-doo!

The riddle with the correct
punctuation is 4.

6

1.
What do you get
if you cross an
alarm clock and
a chicken?

4.
What do you
get if, you cross
an alarm clock
and a
chicken?

3

2.
What do you
get if you cross
an alarm clock,
and a
chicken?

3.
What do you get
if you cross an alarm
clock and a chicken!

Which riddle has the correct punctuation?

Write the number here: _____

3

Great Grammar Mini-Books Scholastic Professional Books

5

Which riddle has the correct punctuation?
Write the number here: _____

3.
What do you get if
you cross, a rooster,
a poodle, and a
cocker spaniel.

2.
What do you
get if you
cross a rooster
a poodle and
a cocker
spaniel?

5.
get if you
cross, a
poodle, and
a cocker
spaniel?

4.
What do you
get if you cross
a rooster, a
poodle and a
cocker spaniel?

1.
What do you get if
you cross a rooster
a poodle, and a
cocker spaniel?

4

The riddle with the correct
punctuation is 1.

An alarm cluck!

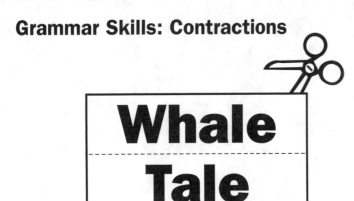

Whale Tale

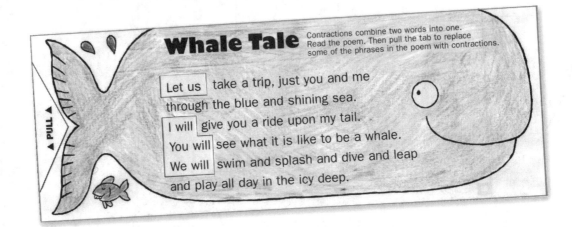

Whale Tale Contractions combine two words into one. Read the poem. Then pull the tab to replace some of the phrases in the poem with contractions.

▲ PULL ▲

Let us take a trip, just you and me
through the blue and shining sea.
I will give you a ride upon my tail.
You will see what it is like to be a whale.
We will swim and splash and dive and leap
and play all day in the icy deep.

Preparation

Provide each student with single-sided photocopies of pattern pages A and B (page 46 and 47). Students also need scissors, tape, and markers or crayons for coloring the book.

Teaching Tips

Review the rule for forming contractions before assembling these "slider" mini-books. The basic rule is: A contraction is formed by putting together two words with certain letters left out. An apostrophe (') is used in place of the missing letters. Write some examples of contractions on the board, and ask students if they can name the letters that are missing in each one.

After students have constructed the mini-books, encourage them to suggest what contractions might be substituted for the five pronoun/predicate phrases visible through the windows. Students can then pull on the whale's tail to reveal the correct contractions.

How to Make the Mini-Book:

1. Place pattern page A on the desk with the printed side facing up. Snip along the solid lines at the bottom of the page, creating two V-shaped cuts.

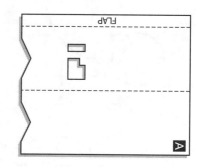

2. Create two "windows" by carefully cutting along the solid lines in the poem.

3. Fold the page in half horizontally along the dashed line.

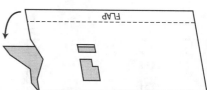

4. Cut out panel B from pattern page B along the solid lines.

5. Slide panel B inside the folded pattern page A. The words "Let us," "I will," "You will," and "We will" should be visible through the cut windows.

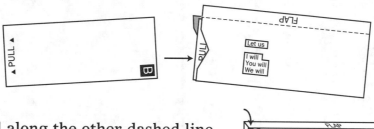

6. Fold along the other dashed line to create a flap. Tape the flap to the back of the page A.

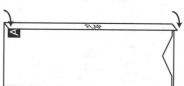

7. Pull on the panel at the whale's tail to transform pronoun/predicate phrases into contractions.

Whale Tale

Contractions combine two words into one. Read the poem. Then pull the tab to replace some of the phrases in the poem with contractions.

take a trip, just you and me

through the blue and shining sea.

give you a ride upon my tail.

see what it is like to be a whale.

swim and splash and dive and leap

and play all day in the icy deep.

FLAP

TAPE FLAP HERE

Great Grammar Mini-Books Scholastic Professional Books

B

Let us   Let's

I will   I'll

You will   You'll

We will   We'll

▼ PULL ▼

Preparation

Provide each student with a photocopy of pattern page A (page 50). Students will also need tape, scissors, and crayons or markers for coloring the books.

Teaching Tips

Explain to students that the possessive form of a noun shows ownership. Review the rules for forming singular and plural possessives before sharing this mini-book "slider" with students.

♦ Most singular nouns add *'s* to become possessive.

♦ A plural noun ending in *s* simply adds an apostrophe (') to become possessive.

♦ A plural noun ending in a letter other than *s* (*children, women, sheep,* etc.) adds *'s* to become possessive.

Ask the class to create two lists on the chalkboard. One list should include all the single possessives on the mini-book slider; the other should include all the plural possessives on the slider. Encourage students to add additional examples of singular and plural possessives to the lists.

To Make the Mini-Book

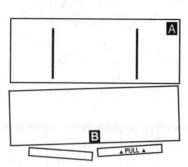

1. Have students cut along the solid lines on the pattern page to separate pet shop panel A, people panel B, and the two pull tabs. The panels should be faceup on the desk.

2. Carefully cut along the two vertical solid lines on panel A to create two slits.

3. Tape the blank tab to the left end of panel B.

4. Push the right end (the one without the tab) of panel B through the slit on the left side of the pet shop on panel A. Pull panel B through the slit and across the back of panel A. Then poke the end of panel B back up through the slit on the right side of the pet shop.

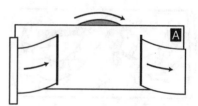

5. Now tape the pull-tab to the right end of panel B as shown.

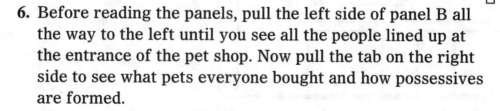

6. Before reading the panels, pull the left side of panel B all the way to the left until you see all the people lined up at the entrance of the pet shop. Now pull the tab on the right side to see what pets everyone bought and how possessives are formed.

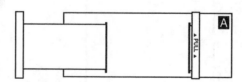

Possessives show ownership. Pull the tab to see who takes home which pet.

Pete's Pet Shop

Did you know?

- Most single noun possessives end in 's.

- Most plural noun possessives end in s'.

Great Grammar Mini-Books Scholastic Professional Books

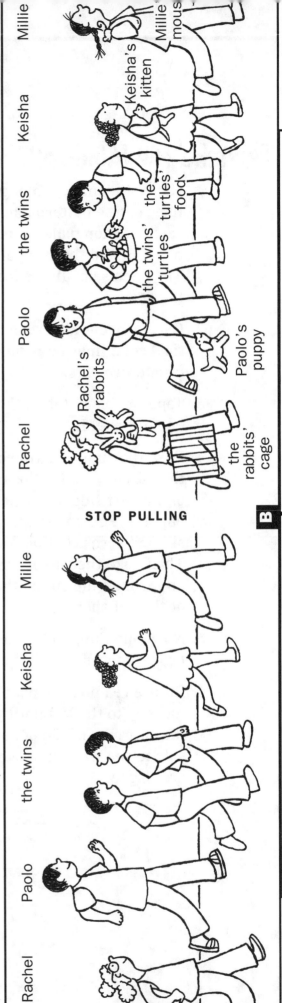

Rachel   Paolo   the twins   Keisha   Millie

Rachel's rabbits

the rabbits' cage

Paolo's puppy

the twins' turtles

the twins' turtles' food

Keisha's kitten

Millie's mouse

STOP PULLING

Rachel   Paolo   the twins   Keisha   Millie

▲ PULL ▲

The Runaway Sentence

Preparation

Provide each student with a double-sided photocopy of the pattern pages 53 and 54. Students will also need scissors, tape, and crayons or markers to color the books.

Teaching Tips

Explain to students that a sentence is a group of words that expresses a complete thought. Use the following examples to illustrate the difference between a sentence and a fragment.

♦ When I'm ready to go. (fragment)

♦ I'll call you when I'm ready to go. (sentence)

Now write the sentences below on the board. Ask students to identify the number of complete thoughts each contains. Tell students that these are examples of *run-on sentences*. A run-on sentence contains more than one complete thought. Ask students to suggest ways to break the run-on sentences into two separate sentences.

♦ I put my shoes on, I'm ready to go.

♦ Don't forget your umbrella, it might rain and then what would you do.

After students explore run-on sentences further in the mini-book, you may want to point out that not all run-on sentences are long. Write the sentences below on the board and ask students how they can be broken down or amended with a semicolon or conjunction.

♦ Let go it's mine.

♦ I'm tired I'm going to bed.

♦ Where is my book I need it.

To Make the Mini-Book

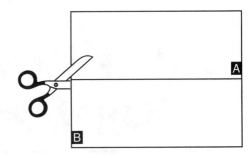

1. Trim the strips marked on each side of the page. Then cut along the solid line to separate panels A and B.

2. Begin with panel A. Place the panel on the desk so that the side with the dashed lines is faceup. Fold the panel in half along the center dashed line. Crease well and unfold.

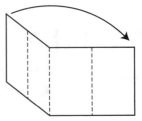

3. Flip the panel over. Fold the right edge and the left edge of the panel in to meet the center fold, folding along the vertical dashed lines on the reverse side. Crease well and unfold.

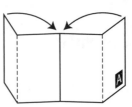

4. Repeat steps 2 and 3 with panel B.

5. Tape the end of panel A to the end of panel B, so that the squares line up.

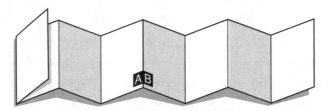

6. Fold the pages back and forth along the creases to create an accordion book.

7. To read, unfold the accordion book panel by panel.

TRIM OFF THIS STRIP.

The Runaway Sentence

Woof!

Hold on tight.
It's going to be
quite a ride!

3

Great Grammar Mini-Books Scholastic Professional Books

TRIM OFF THIS STRIP.

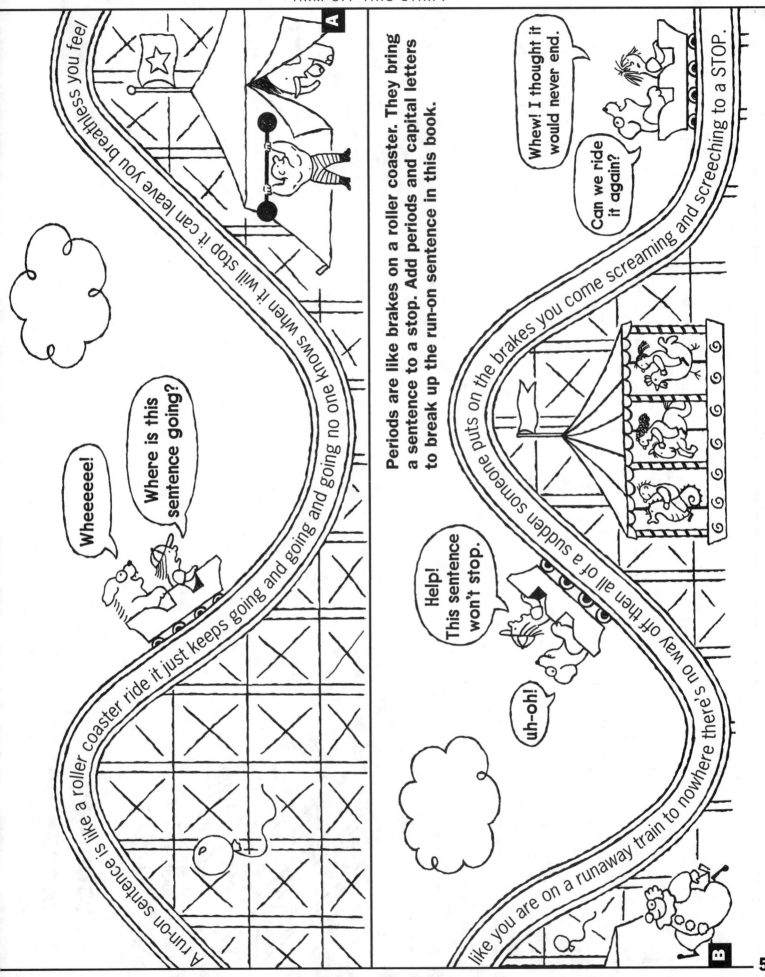

Periods are like brakes on a roller coaster. They bring a sentence to a stop. Add periods and capital letters to break up the run-on sentence in this book.

Preparation

Provide each student with photocopies of pattern pages A, B, and E (pages 57, 58, 61) and a double-sided photocopy of pattern pages C and D (pages 59 and 60). Students will also need scissors, a stapler, a pencil, and markers or crayons for coloring the book.

Teaching Tips

Review with students the rules of capitalization before assembling and reading the mini-book. You may want to pay particular attention to how to distinguish between proper nouns and common nouns, as this distinction will be important as students embark on their mini-book "treasure hunt."

Words that take capital letters include:

♦ the first word in a sentence

♦ proper nouns

♦ the pronoun *I*

To Make the Mini-Book

1. Cut along the solid lines on pattern page A to create pointed flaps.

2. Fold the bottom section of the pattern UP along the horizontal dashed line.

3. Staple along the right and left edges of the folded part of the pattern to create a long pocket.

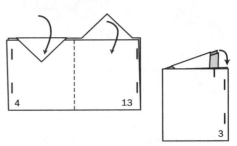

4. Fold the two pointed flaps DOWN along the dashed lines.

5. Fold the pattern in half along the vertical dashed line. Set the folded panel aside.

6. Repeat steps 1–5 with pattern page B.

7. Cut along the three horizontal solid lines on pattern page C. You should have two panels.

8. Fold the panels in half along the vertical dashed lines.

9. You now have four folded panels. Nest them together so that the pages are in numerical order. Staple the book along the left edge to hold the pages in place.

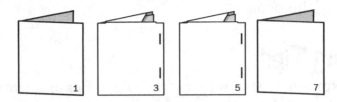

10. Cut along the solid lines on pattern page E. You should have four clues labeled 1–4.

11. Pages 3, 5, 10, and 12 of the mini-book form envelope pockets. Slip the four clues in these pockets, matching the number of the clue with the number on the envelope flap.

12. As you read the mini-book, pull out the clues contained in each of the envelope pockets.

Open the envelope for clue #4.

Open the envelope for clue #1.

Penny and Percy studied the clues. "Look!" Penny said. "Some of these words should have capital letters. If we put the letters together, I bet we'll crack the code and learn the location of the treasure chest."

Then one day, Paul decided he was tired of being a pirate. So he bid his pirate pals farewell. As Paul was leaving, he told his friends about a hidden treasure chest.

14

3

13

4

7

Open the envelope
for clue #3.

Open the envelope
for clue #2.

Percy and Penny walked for miles until they came to the town. The envelope was just where Paul said it would be.

"You have to find the treasure yourselves, but here's a clue to get you started," he told his friends. He handed them an envelope. "So long!"

12

5

11

9

5

AL'S ANTIQUES

16

TREASURE HUNT

1

They climbed ashore and saw a big X in the sand. They dug and dug. Instead of a treasure chest, they found another clue.

10

Great Grammar Mini-Books Scholastic Professional Books

Penny and Percy did what the letter said. When they came to the ship, they found another envelope taped to its mast.

7

9
→

Once there were three pirates. Their names were Penny, Paul, and Percy. They had a happy life sailing the seas and searching for treasure.

2

See if you're as clever as Penny and Percy. Look at the clues. Circle all the letters that should be capitalized. Put the letters together. What do they spell? Write your answer here. Then turn the page to see if you're right.

15

Percy and Penny sailed across the stormy sea, just like the letter told them to do.

8

In a few days, they reached the island.

9

Great Grammar Mini-Books Scholastic Professional Books

Dear Penny and Percy,

Walk down Albany avenue. Turn right at lucy's Cafe and head for the harbor. Look for a ship named the salty Dog.

Your pal,
Paul

Clue #1

Dear Penny and Percy,

Sail the Salty Dog across the atlantic Ocean around Cape nelson. Continue past treasure Cove until you reach Annabelle island. Remember, X marks the spot!

Ahoy,
Paul

Clue #2

Dear Pirate Pals,

Head north until you reach a tiny town. Turn left at quigly's Drugstore. under the bridge, you'll find the final clue.

Bye,
Paul

Clue #3

Dear P&P,

Well, you're almost there. But I don't want to make it too easy for you. each clue I've given you contains part of a secret code. see if you can crack it. It will tell you where to find the treasure.

Good luck,
Paul

Clue #4

NOTES:

NOTES:

NOTES: